BPD

To Poohpaw (Michael Addison, my stepdad) thank
you for being there for me so many nights during
the many mental health crisis' over the years. Thank
you for being with me throughout and never judging
me for being crazy. And to the Counsellors,
Psychiatrists and Nurses who helped me get where I
am today with my mental health.

Thank you Alli Hunter for editing and Sonya
Guingona for the illustrations

AUTHORS NOTE:

This book of poetry touches on some dark topics. It can be overwhelming if you are not in the right head space! Please consume safely. Please read the trigger warnings on the next page!

<u>Table of contents</u>

<u>Section three</u>: On Journal Prompts.

<u>Section Four</u>: On death and suicide.

<u>Section Five</u>: On living with mental Illness.

Section one: On What I Wish I Had Said.

My Dear Watson

Since the day you left, I've been trying to put pen to paper, to tell you how sorry I am, but ink blots replaced words on those pages.

They said it was a simple procedure, but you might have to stay overnight.

Your eyes pleaded with me to stay, but my ride needed to get to a party, and I had exams to study for. If I had known it would turn out like this, I never would have left your side, would have made the most of the time I had left with you.

Instead, I kissed you one last time and left you with the doctor, expecting to see you in a few hours' time.

Now instead, the colour black is not dark enough to describe the void

I feel without you by my side.

The doctor called it a complication, an unforeseen circumstance, that the muscle in your heart must have been damaged because it stopped beating. Just like mine when they told me, and it's funny because just days before we were curled up in my bed and I could hear your heart beat, it was alive and strong.

We had only known each other for a year and a half, were only really together those last few months, and I am sorry I tried to replace you. It was more about me then you. This void that takes up space, even now, that I desperately want to fill.

But, I know deep down I never could, because you were so precious to me, and I don't know if I will find that kind of love again, but I know I am looking for it in all the wrong places.

My dear Watson, can you ever forgive me for breaking the way I did? Crumbling to pieces, while crushing those around me. For destroying what little good we had built together.

My dear Watson, what I am trying to say is: I love you.

How Dare You

You called me selfish, spoiled,

and a whole litany of other names

over 1.99$.

Except it wasn't 1.99$,

you've been wanting rid of me since you met me,

deemed me unworthy of your presence,

because I was nothing like you.

You could have just said you didn't want to be
friends,

instead, you insult me, demean me and try to destroy my other friendships?

Don't you know I've dealt with your kind before?

Don't you know that I'm bulletproof from those words?

Don't you know I could have taken you down if I wanted to?

Destroyed you like I did the last person who did that to me?

Instead, I chose to ignore you, not stoop down to your pathetic level,

I know that hurting others because they hurt me is not worth it,

because I know karma is a bitch and she's coming for you.

Monster Manual

Today I flipped through a book, and was surprised, flabbergasted, not to see your name nor your picture.

I tried a similar book, then another, and another, but still nothing. So, in desperation I bought one called the Monster Manual. Expecting to see you under E or similar,

But, to my immense horror, you weren't there, though you so belonged.

You weren't there, even though you're the most horrible, wicked, and vindictive monster I have had the displeasure of knowing in this lifetime.

Given the choice of spending one minute in your presence, or rotting in a dark, monster-filled, putrid-smelling, running-for-my-life labyrinth that I will never escape, I would 100% choose the labyrinth. Even if it was always night, and I could hear the monsters slowly closing in on me.

Would that make a person think twice about choosing you?

Would it make them stumble and question why I would choose certain horror-filled death over you?

Why are those monsters less monstrous than you?

It's simply because you are the worst kind of monster there is.

FUCK YOU!

I am Enough

I want to tell you that you will be enough and that I myself am enough

But sometimes I am an empty bookshelf because I don't want to read anymore. That all my books are scattered on the floor, half open like this poem I am trying to write.

Sometimes telling yourself I am enough is not enough. Sometimes you need to reach out before you shatter, and are nothing more than books on the floor left to rot.

Sometimes we are not beautiful poetry, but the scars left behind after we have walked through the fire, we set alight.

We are not the flowers that bloom against adversity. We are broken and afraid.

So, listen when I tell you I am not enough to save myself, even if I have to be

Ace And in Need of SPACE

I loved the idea of you, and I'm sorry,

I was trying to be someone they wanted me to be...

I don't want to have that white picket fence home
with a husband, 2.5 kids.

I loved that they thought I was normal when I was
with you,

How they stopped questioning if something was
wrong with me,

You slowly picked at me until I couldn't stand
myself,

You pulled up every scab, telling me the way I
loved wasn't good enough,

That I would never make it work,

I was hardly a shell of a person, and I couldn't do that to myself again.

So, I chose myself over you and I would do it,

OVER AND OVER AGAIN.

I will proudly be the rainbow sheep of the family,

Because my feeling of self-worth trumps their idea that Eros was necessary for me to live.

It is not a part of me and never will be.

We are tragic lovers,

Always to be torn apart,

Our love, always fleeting

Some nights I crave your sweet embrace,

But it does not come. You leave me frozen

Some nights I take other lovers,

Less tragic, they keep me warm

In your hollow absence

And yes, I miss your sweet embrace

Like it once was, But now

you are a hollow ache, and stiff neck

In the morning.

You are what I wanted, but instead you broke

Us, you, and me

I will always want your warm embrace,

How you kept me safe from the monsters that lurk,

And the dangers I know all too well.

We are tragic lovers because our love, so pure, will

be ripped away, again and again.

YOU KNOW WHO YOU ARE!!!

FUCKING DAMN IT DAVE

Not Dave, but you,

Who will never read this, and that's fine

It isn't meant for you. It's meant for me, and those

who lost their power

Whose power you took.

This is for those whom you still hold power over

And those who are still looking for their power.

I want to say I'm sorry, I didn't destroy you, when I

had the chance.

That I let someone else feel what I felt, scared and alone.

I don't want another person to feel like this,

I will advocate for anything, for their healing,

I will draft poem after poem, if it helps one person heal

From people the likes of you

I will focus on the healing and not the hate,

even though sometimes it sneaks in,

and dips its' toes in our brains',

our first response to something is how we are

conditioned to think.

But, Our second thought is how we truly feel,

So, I may feel hate because it is conditioned

but I truly feel love, because that is what is needed.

Section Two: When Emotions Run High

Kindly Fuck off, Yours truly <3

This is the last I will write of you,

You who are not worthy of being remembered even

though you live.

I just wanted to say that I CAN & I WILL

That I got that tattoo you told me to never get, then

I got ten more,

Because they make me feel pretty.

Because, my body is a temple, I am the goddess that it is dedicated to. And I will decorate it how I want, for it is my temple, not yours.

I cut my hair short, and gained some weight because you told me you didn't want me to get fat.

I started dyeing my bangs different colours even though you said it was tacky,

I told myself I CAN & I WILL, I loved it so much I wrote it on me permanently,

I pierced my ears so many times I lost count, and scowled at those who told me to smile.

I burned sage to get your negativity off me, and that was a lifesaver, but I needed to write these poems to finish the cleanse.

So, this is me telling you, who will never read this, even if I publish it, that I got along without you just fine.

Hell, I excelled without you.

So kindly stick your head in a bucket of ice water.
<3

__Rage__

Every tear is just the infancy,

Of the incoming storm.

My rage will not be quelled

With your passive words

And lack of action.

My rage is as mighty as a mountain

And just as solid too.

It burns like a wild fire

That you are so desperate to put out.

My feelings are not delicate like butterflies' wings,
easily ripped to shreds,

My feelings are delicate like lava, burning everything in its wake

The Same Pain

FUCK YOU GOSH DAMN IT.

 We did not feel the same pain,

you were waiting for a chance,

and I was vulnerable.

You said I hurt you,

BUT, WHAT THE HELL DID I DO?

Well, what did I do?

 You can't tell me.

You said it was my fault.

How was you breaking up with me,

with a bitter storyline, you concocted yourself,

my fucking fault?

I know you were jealous I went drinking without you.

But should I remind you what the hell happened when you got drunk?

That was a thousand times worse

Be happy I fucking fought,

and was ignorant enough to not break up with you.

Because if you pulled that same shit now,

you would have a broken nose among other things

So, we did not feel the same pain.

Mine was an excruciating inferno,

yours was a piddly, minor burn.

__Throne of Lies.__

Do not sit on my throne of lies

And claim them as your own,

I will fight you to the last breath.

This facade, this carefully crafted throne of what I
am, and am not, is mine alone.

You do not belong here,

The guards should not have let you in,

I am too powerful to fall to my knees and ask you
for forgiveness for my own mistakes.

So, move before I shove you off of what little I have
left.

Leave me to wither away, on my throne of lies

I Spilled The Tea

I spilled the tea, all over myself.

Making me look a fool.

I spilled it, and I can't put it back.

Why was I such a tool?

I spilled the tea, and it's everywhere.

I didn't think I was so cruel,

The tea is spilled and the matter is done.

If I don't clean it up, I will just add fuel.

I Do Not Write Happy Poetry

I do not write happy poetry.

It does not come to me at happy times but times of distress, anger and sadness.

I wish I could write you a happy poem,

I've tried so many times but the words don't leave my lips exactly right like the burnt marshmallow.

I will burn before being the golden person.

My poetry is pain and brutality, the suffering I feel in everyday life it is my bipolar and anxiety and depression all bundled into one. It is not pretty. It will never be pretty.

It was never meant to be pretty it is meant to be honest. And that is all I will ask for it to be raw.

Section Three: On Journal Prompts

When is The Use of Violence Justified?

I could argue this, seven ways from Sunday,

each with little notes and arguments for support,

I took Philosophy after all,

but we should first ask what kind of violence?

the kind that hurts just me or you?

Or us, or them?

The kind that kills, or maims, or hurts our hearts?

Because words too, are a kind of violence, that stays
a long time.

If it kills then what can justify reaping the life of a
person who simply existed,

would you offer up your life for another?

If you just meant to maim, did you know that they
are a person too? They exist in the same time, in the

same world as yours, so why would you try and ruin something so sacred?

If you think just words of violence are okay, would you like them said to you with the same intent? If they settle in your heart the same

My argument is this, the world would be a beautiful place without violence, but to be a world without violence

We must first heal the violence in our hearts.

What do You Need to Forgive Yourself For?

It's not simple, not really

I do not need to apologize for crying,

or for fighting back.

I do not need to apologize for being human,

but I do need to apologize for putting myself
through hell,

For something I could not control.

for something someone else did,

for hurting myself,

for swallowing those pills,

for putting shields up so high I couldn't see the light

of dawn,

of the next day.

Of the life I could live

I need to apologize to myself for that because,

there is a light at the end of the tunnel, it may be piddly.

But, it is here and we have reached it

It Wasn't Meant to go This Far, I Swear.

If it wasn't then why did it?

Why was I left in the cold,

bruised and battered with a knife to my throat?

Scared of even leaving these four walls?

Cause it sure as hell feels like you meant to.

It wasn't meant to go this far I swear?

Sounds like a lie you told the cops to get out of trouble.

To this day those words swim through my mind
occasionally,

If it wasn't meant to go this fucking far, why do you sit
smirking?

Like you got away with murder,

cause you almost did, but I'm the only one who knows,

You almost did.

Does War Make Monsters or do Monsters Make War?

Does war make monsters, or do monsters make war?

They will tell you the location of every star in the sky.

How they are counting the days to see you

They will make it sound like they never left

But inside the darkness is churning,

Slowly eating away at what is left of my sanity

Trying to stay just one step ahead of it

Forgetting the sound of a firing gun is not so easy

Their hands calloused from working and in working their gun.

<u>Are We Alone In The Universe?</u>

Alone in our minds,

sometimes left alone,

but we are not alone.

Even if we feel it now,

somewhere in this universe,

there is someone we can call a friend.

Even if it is an alien from Mars.

Advice On What Matters Most.

I sat and pondered what I wanted to say.

Many things came to mind, and at the same time, I was stumped.

I want to say the people I care about, or is that too obvious

And I don't mean a partner because we don't actually need one...

Or so I at least seem to think, I've been happier thus far without a relationship compared to one.

Maybe I am just happier without a male partner.

All of the cats and dogs and chinchillas matter too,

Maybe I should say peace?

That is important both in the worldly sense and the personal one.

Worldly peace, free of violence, and intolerance is important.

But personal peace, from the violence of the mind is important too.

Being able to get up and feel confident in "I can do this".

Or being happy with decisions you make like kids or no kids,

ALLLLL the fur babies or a career that makes you happy like law or pottery?

Being Happy makes the list, being happy makes the top of the list.

Section Four: *On Death and Suicide*

I Miss You.

I will stand here and I will not say a word because I have no words left to say.

You promised it was going to be okay.

That I wasn't going to feel this hurt just yet, so let me stand here and say nothing, because the pain of your absence created a much deeper hole then I expected.

Took too much from my already fragile heart. So, I will stand here, and let my silence speak volumes. Or, better yet, listen to what my tears have to say as they slide down my cheeks.

Listen to the rage in my fists, as I sink my nails deeper, while everyone tells me I will be okay.

I am not, nor will I be anytime soon, because you can't just get over loss like that. It's like scar tissue it takes time healing, and when it's done it's never the same as before.

If it were the same as before you would be here, and I wouldn't be like this. I didn't ask to be like this, as I've told you a million times. I did not ask to be like this. You made me this.

Pills

My days and my nights start the same

With a small handful of multicolored pills.

It has been this way for a while and

I can't remember a time when I didn't take them,

Except when I stopped, but that is a whole other
black hole I don't want to invite you through.

Not quite yet anyway.

The pills all have their purpose, to make me sleep,
to wake me up, to make me happy, and to make me
not quite too happy.

What I'm saying is I take a lot of pills, because I got
marked as one in five.

That the thoughts going through your head when I tell you I'm bipolar aren't always kind

That you being one of the four out of five make it hard to understand why my days and nights start like this, or why I even need these chemicals in the first place.

Even though it doesn't hurt you, I hide them when you come over, like dirty dishes.

The pills have a purpose, they make me feel, or feel not so much, and some days that is the best I can ask for

Because some days, the most I can ask of these pills is to feel nothing.

I am sick of being okay against my will.

I want it all to fade into the background like a blur.

I want the loud empty smiles to hush, and the rambling words of those who don't understand what it's like to have this curse to dispense.

I am sick of taking the pills, and following the drills which make me okay.

It's okay to have a sad day,

To fall flat on my face and have nobody catch me. It makes the good days so much more savory.

I can't be okay every day, I can't smile, and sing along to your freaking Kumbaya circle, but I am not okay. My good days are sometimes just less severe bad days, and if I can make it through this, I can make it through anything.

Or maybe I will stop dead center, waiting for something that will never come. Hitting the brakes on this life.

__Fertilizer__

In the end, we are but fertilizer for those yet to come.

We come from the earth and go back to it, contributing to it along the way.

Some become ash and are spread to the four corners of the world,

Some sit whole in little caskets and coffins waiting until they disintegrate,

Leaving nothing but dust, between six and thirty years.

Others are put directly into the dirt, lost to the ages.

Edge of The Abyss

I think if you asked me what I was most afraid of, I
would not say death or dying.

I have hovered on the edge of an abyss for so long I
do not remember what is real anymore.

I have fought and lost so many battles against
myself I may not win the war.

The scariest part is, maybe I don't want to.
Sometimes I want the world to stop spinning so fast
so that just once I can get ahead, and know when
the magic wears off, instead of the surprise of being
set adrift.

Little Orange Pills Were Easier to Swallow Then The Face That You Weren't Coming Back

Nine times in two months I swallowed too many,

Maybe I thought I would see you again.

Maybe I wanted to join you.

But, all I knew, was that I missed you,

and those little orange pills made me feel better.

After all, they were for anxiety.

I thought maybe if I took one more, one more, one more,

that I would miss you less, be less anxious about it anyways.

Nine times in two months, I had to call an ambulance

tell them about my selfish overdose.

Because I decided I didn't want to be gone,

People loved me and I loved them,

So, they took away my pills,

giving me three days at a time.

And God, am I thankful for that,

so damn thankful someone cared.

Thank you if you ever read this.

One More Time.

If I could say I love you one more time,
I would say it a billion.

If I could hug you again,
I would squeeze you as tight as possible.

If only I could hear you, and see you again.
But now you are just ashes in the wind.
An empty body with a free soul.

Good And Bad Days

The struggle with being suicidal at the age of eleven is you never think you're gonna make it to 20 or even 18.

You think one day it will finally be too much and you'll end it.

The pain and suffering and everything will just be over.

A few weeks ago, I turned twenty-three.

I live by myself with my cat, but the thing is some days are good days now.

Some days I spend hours baking. Or playing fetch with my dog. And it feels like the monsters can't get to me anymore.

But the problem is some days I can't get out of bed, and the monsters make appealing reasons why my soul should stop spinning on the earth's axis.

Some days the strongest thing I can do is take my pills and hope the screaming stops.

The thing is at least I have those good days.

Section Five: On living with mental Illness.

<u>**Insomnia**</u>

As I lay awake near dawn,

Where sleep is a mere dream,

I wonder if my psychiatrist knows,

The insomnia is not from naps or lack of pills,

Which they seem to be itching to shove down my throat.

That the psychosis is not from the insomnia.

No, the psychosis came from somewhere else, somewhere unfamiliar to me, somewhere I can't touch, but voices I can hear. Pestering me,

Provoking me, silencing me.

The insomnia is fear of those voices getting into my head. Those voices are showing me where they are from, and I do not want to go.

For the only thing I know about it, is that it is far past the land of the living.

<u>Undertow</u>

It's like being caught in the undertow, constantly trying to get out, get one more breath before it sweeps you away.

Life is like a bullet train, that never stops, even though it is making you nauseous, and giving you a migraine.

It is a never relenting force that is always, always trying to drag you along with it, even if you need a moment to collect yourself, change your shirt because it is stained with coffee, or collect those files that someone you love knocked down in a hurry.

Life is not going to pause for you so pause for it. Take a second out of your day and breathe. Inhale slowly and exhale even slower, until that feeling of urgency, of panic, of being completely overwhelmed subsides, just for a second, just for you. That second of pure bliss.

The Axe

My emotions swing both ways like an axe.

Both deadly, but changing the destination.

Me or you, me or you?

Who will get hit this time?

Who will get hurt?

Will my depression hurt me like a bad dice roll?

Or will it hurt you like an out-of-control forest fire?

I am never sure what will happen, and I am scared.

For both are dreadfully painful,

and I wish neither would happen.

But they do, and I can only brace for impact.

The shadows are speaking to me

As you slumber, I wake.

Striding through these empty hallways,

looking aimlessly for someone,

but they have disappeared long ago.

Leaving behind only shadows of what could have been,

they speak to me, whispering sweet nothings in my ear,

calling me into the shadows to take me away.

The shadows call out to me "Come here, I'm here"

but I know I should not listen.

For they are not you,

but what you left behind to taunt me.
Their whispers sound so appealing,

As the night goes on,

they grow more desperate.

Enticing me to come with them,

and I think I just might.

Disappearing into the shadows sounds better with
you,

than here, stalking the halls all alone.

Against My Better Judgement

I can't count on all my fingers and toes,

How many times have I blinded myself from the truth?

How I lied to myself, not because of love or such foolishness,

but because my brain lied to me.

Because I lied to it,

that I was mentally okay to go.

To do stuff that would hurt me,

against my better judgment,

means something different

when mental illness is involved.

Everything is hazy,

judgment is impaired,

and lines are crossed that shouldn't be,

Against my better judgment, I was friends with you after all?

Against my better judgment, I kept drinking after all.

Against my better judgment I tried to die.

<u>That Damn Thing Led me Straight in a Pit.</u>

All my trust went out the window,

AS

    I

       FELL

          INTO

             THAT

                PIT

                   DOWN

              DOWN

        DOWN

DOWN

into that damned pit.

Where I am stuck with me, myself, and I

and that is not a place I want to be.

Being stuck with me, myself, and I

is very unpleasant and unsettling.

Being alone with one's thoughts is the spell for self-destruction.

That damn thing led me here on purpose,

stuck in this pit with no hope of rescue.

You planned this,

leading me out of the town, through the forest,

straight into this pit of despair.

So why did you do it?

Nobody is Coming, You're alone.

That's what I told myself for so, so long.

I felt that way because it was what I was taught to feel.

I thought I was alone when I wanted to die,

When I wanted to stop feeling this pain,

This dull ache that never went away.

Nobody is coming, is what I told myself

when I swallowed that first pill,

then the next twenty or so.

You're alone, nobody is coming,

as I puked up every single one of them,

burning my throat, as I puked again and again,

until I felt empty.

I didn't puke because I wanted to,

the pills had a coating that if you take too many

it makes you sick.

I curled up in bed afterward, hiding what I did.

Ten years later, nobody knew what I did,

nobody came, I was alone.

But,

that doesn't mean I am alone today.

Section Six: On choosing me.

Nobody Came, But I am Not Alone.

Between eleven and twenty was the worst of my
depression.

I was constantly on the verge of disappearing
through the cracks.

The cracks that seemed so small to everyone else,

were so big and welcoming to me.

Nobody came for me at that time,

but I am no longer alone.

I have friends who at my lowest,

ask me are you okay?

 And mean it

Thank you for that,

I wish I could explain how much that warms my
heart

How long it took to find my people,

despite how splintered they are.

These glorious people helped me rise from the ashes
like

a phoenix,

until I no longer saw the cracks as welcoming,

but as tiny insignificant cracks.

So, nobody came at first, but I am not alone

I Choose Me, I Will Always Choose Me

I have never been so in love,

That I was willing to rip myself in half

to be with them.

Never felt a love so intense,

that it was necessary.

And I wonder why people do this?

Where is the self-love to put yourself together,

the self-love to rip out their guts for your own.

Because in the end, you truly have only yourself to
love.

We have never met, but we know each other so well, that we are mistaken for each other.

I'll Never be That me Again

I may never be her again

and for that, I am devastated.

Devastated I couldn't save her days of despair and
rot in her little head.

Devastated by the choices she made and the despair
she felt,

Devastated by the world bearing down its weight on
her small body.

Devastated that she lost out on so much because of
cruel people.

Devastated that nobody reached out their hand to
her.

But I did.

I re-taught her how to smile even if it started in the mirror, mimicking someone.

I re-taught her to laugh even though it sounded like wheezing before a chortle.

I taught her that she could step on other people's toes because her happiness mattered too.

I am her, and though I wish I could have saved her earlier,

I am happy that I will never be that me again.

Ace and Tired of Your Shit.

Falling asleep is considered to be a sweet embrace.

Of what?

I have no fucking clue.

I'm Asexual and sex repulsed.

So, sex is disgusting, and being embraced is gross

This is my poem, I make the rules.

So, falling asleep is like being ushered into a good book

The first few steps of an all-out 100 m run,

It takes a moment, but when you get there, it's more than satisfying,

it's Enthralling,

The utter disrespect my body has, even with sleeping pills, of the time it takes to fall asleep

is downright appalling, but the journey is not as important as the destination.

The destination of entering my dreams, a mostly safe space where anything is almost possible

Nightmares and stories to be told lurk around every corner.

No sweet embrace here,

actually

DON'T

FUCKING

TOUCH

ME!

I will warn you once, I sure as hell don't bite but I do stab.

So sweet embrace? HA NO! I'll take the 100 m run instead.

On love

Take your time,

Hold their eye contact for an extra second before
that first kiss, or the thousandth one.

Hold their hand even if your hand is sweaty.

Trust me they won't mind.

Take your time to fall in love it's a marathon not a
sprint.

Take the time to get to know them,

The good and the bad.

Like the way their dimples come out when they
smile wide, or they furrow their brow in frustration
when they keep dying in their video game.

Never settle for enough, go for grand.

Fall for the bad boy, but know if he keeps hurting you to walk away, it's not love

Strive for success even when you and everyone else is telling you you're bound for failure. Go back to school at 25, 50, or 80, if you're not in love with what you're doing. Never feel ashamed to cry or get angry. It's how we know we're still human. Sometimes it's the only thing that makes us feel human.

Butcher Block

How long do I have to scream?

Until it's too bloodcurdling to watch?

How long until you leave me alone to be in my peace

Inside of the horror story, I got stuck in with you?

I guess I have to stop screaming like a victim

Instead, I must pull a knife out of a wooden butcher block,

And chase you until you can't run.

You're hiding, hand blocking your mouth in case any air escapes.

Fighting back tears and lungs burning,

waiting for my footsteps

To

    Completely

      Disa-

          -PEAR? OH NO baby, you're
not surviving this time, I'm getting my peace.

Message to the Moon

Often our paths cross, mostly on purpose.

But like your dark side, I am often hidden from view,

As I lurk the aisles of my job.

Other times we are companions as I write, or read,

or go on adventures through foreign lands without leaving my place.

We are comrades, one is rarely seen without the other, we are not two ships passing in the night,

We are often the silhouette of each other, when one of us is gone, the other disappears in comradery.

We have never met, but we know each other so well, that we are mistaken for each other.

Printed in the USA
CPSIA information can be obtained
at www.ICGtesting.com
LVHW031050021224
797971LV00058B/180